Clever CREATURES
Anne Rooney

Badger Publishing Limited
Oldmedow Road,
Hardwick Industrial Estate,
King's Lynn PE30 4JJ
Telephone: 01438 791037

www.badgerlearning.co.uk

2 4 6 8 10 9 7 5 3

Clever Creatures ISBN 978-1-78464-101-6

Text © Anne Rooney 2015

Complete work © Badger Publishing Limited 2015

All rights reserved. No part of this publication may be reproduced, stored in any form or by any means mechanical, electronic, recording or otherwise without the prior permission of the publisher.

The right of Anne Rooney to be identified as author of this work has been asserted by her in accordance with the Copyright, Designs and Patents Act 1988.

Publisher: Susan Ross
Senior Editor: Danny Pearson
Publishing Assistant: Claire Morgan
Designer: Fiona Grant
Series Consultant: Dee Reid

Photos: Cover Image: Eye Ubiquitous/REX
Page 5: © Relaximages / Alamy
Page 6: © blickwinkel/Alamy
Page 8: Geoff Moore/REX
Page 9: © Arterra Picture Library/Alamy
Page 11: FLPA/REX
Page 12: Gerard Lacz/REX
Page 13: FLPA/REX
Page 14: Image Broker/REX
Page 15: Russian Look/UIG/REX
Page 16: John Cancalosi/Nature Picture/REX
Page 17: David Kjaer/ Nature Picture L/REX
Page 18: FLPA/Gianpiero Ferrari/REX
Page 19: Design Pics Inc/REX
Page 20: Design Pics Inc/REX
Page 21: © WENN Ltd/Alamy
Page 22: Geoff Moore/REX
Page 23: FLPA/REX
Page 25: © D. Hurst/Alamy
Page 26: © dpa picture alliance/Alamy
Page 27: © dpa picture alliance/Alamy
Page 28: K Tornblom/IBL/REX
Page 29: FLPA/Dave Pressland/REX
Page 30: Anup Shah/Fiona Rogers/REX

Attempts to contact all copyright holders have been made.
If any omitted would care to contact Badger Learning, we will be happy to make appropriate arrangements.

Contents

1. All together, now!	6
2. Master builders	10
3. Looking after baby	16
4. Super smart!	20
5. Problem solving	26
Questions	31
Index	32

Vocabulary

apartments   primates
communicate   recognise
expensive   sequence
fibre   successful

Humans are the most successful animals on the planet.

There are reasons for this:

- Our hands are free because we walk on our back legs.

- We have thumbs, which make our hands more useful than paws.

But humans aren't the only clever ones! There are lots of creatures that can do amazing things.

1. All Together, Now!

It's always smart to work with others to tackle a hard task. Even some tiny animals know that.

Smart ants

One type of ant makes themselves into a chain to carry large items, such as dead millipedes.

Some types of ants work together to carry away really big creatures such as birds, bats or even snakes.

If flood waters reach a fire ants' nest they have a really clever trick. The ants use their legs and jaws to hook on to each other to form themselves into a living raft.

The raft is flat and floats on water so the ants can load their eggs and young onto the raft to keep them safe.

It only works because every ant does its job.

Making rain

Seagulls usually eat fish when they are by the sea, but many seagulls don't live beside the sea. How can they find food?

Some have a really clever trick! They land on a field and all stamp their feet at the same time.

The worms that live underground think it's raining. They come to the surface, and the seagulls gobble them up.

Ring of bubbles

Whales have a clever trick to catch food. A group of up to 12 whales circles a shoal of fish.

They blow a ring of bubbles that the fish won't swim through. Some whales blow bubbles, and other whales keep the fish together.

Then the whales close in, making the ring smaller and smaller.

At last, they storm the ring and feast on the fish.

WOW! facts

Sperm whales have the largest brain of any creature, at 7.8 kilograms.

2. MASTER BUILDERS

Humans live in all types of homes:
- igloos
- tents
- log cabins
- brick houses

Animals live in all types of homes, too. Some are cleverly built and some are rather odd.

Moving in

Most animals have to make their own homes, but some are lazier – or smarter!

The hermit crab lives in a seashell left behind by another animal. The front of the crab is like any other crab – it has a hard shell and strong pincers. But the back end is soft and unprotected.

There is a hermit crab in Legoland, England, that lives in a shell made of Lego.

As the crab grows, it has to find a bigger shell. When it finds one, it moves quickly out of its old shell and into the new one.

Nice nests

Most birds make nests, but some nest-builders are very clever.

Male weaver birds make nests from leaf fibres or grass. They weave the fibres into strange and beautiful shapes to form unusual homes.

Some types of weaver birds work together to build large nests. There are several apartments inside for different bird families.

Nastier nests

The swiftlet doesn't go to the trouble of finding leaves or sticks. Over 35 days, it spits out sticky goo that hardens into strings.

It builds up a nest, shaped like a cup, from its own spit. Would you want to sleep in a bed made from dried spit?

In China, people make soup from these spit nests – it's very expensive!

Towering termites

Termites are insects a bit like ants. They live in huge families. The termites work together to build a mound. The mound has different rooms inside.

It even has tunnels to bring cool air from outside into the mound. Termites build their mounds facing north–south to make the most of the wind.

A mound can be three metres tall and hold two to three million termites.

Paper homes

Not everybody likes wasps, but a wasp nest is a beautiful thing.

Wasps make their nests by chewing up wood or plant fibre to make paper.

The outside of the nest is a ball made from swirls of paper. Inside the nest are the six-sided cells where the queen wasp lays her eggs.

3. Looking After Baby

It's hard work looking after a baby. Some animals make it easier by sharing the work. Others cheat.

Lazy parents

The cuckoo mother lays her eggs in nests that belong to other birds.

First, she pushes out one of the other bird's eggs and lays her own egg in its place. The other mother bird thinks that the cuckoo egg is one of her own.

The cuckoo chick hatches first, and often pushes the other eggs out of the nest.

One type of cuckoo lays her eggs in a reed warbler's nest. The baby cuckoo makes a noise like a whole nest of warbler chicks.

The warbler parents keep bringing it food, working hard.

The cuckoo grows huge – but the warblers keep feeding it. They are so busy that they don't have time to lay more eggs.

Fighting back

The Australian fairy wren fights back against the cuckoos. The mother bird sings to the eggs, teaching the babies inside a password.

When they hatch, the wren chicks sing the password and she feeds them. The cuckoo chick doesn't learn the password, so it doesn't get any food.

Don't eat your babies!

Some fish carry their eggs and even their babies in their mouths. This is called 'mouth brooding'.

The adult fish can't eat while it is waiting for the eggs to hatch.

After they have hatched, the babies swim freely – but return to their parent's mouth if there is any danger.

WOW! facts
The cuckoo catfish eats the eggs of a mouth-brooding fish, and lays its own eggs for the fish to look after.

4. Super Smart!

One of the reasons humans have been so successful is that we use tools. But other animals make and use tools, too.

Smart in the sea

You might not expect octopuses to be really clever, but they are.

Octopuses don't have a shell. Their soft bodies are easy for other animals to eat – so octopuses have to work hard to stay safe.

An octopus sometimes collects coconut shells dropped in the sea by people. It piles them up, then climbs on top.

The octopus holds its tentacles straight like stilts. Then it walks along with the stack of coconut shells and puts them somewhere safe.

It uses the shells to hide itself from danger.

Octopuses aren't the only clever sea creatures.

Dolphins are super-smart. Some dolphins pick up sea sponges from the sea-bed and then use them to stir up sand, uncovering things to eat.

Dolphins can also communicate with each other, and recognise themselves in mirrors. They can play, learn tricks and even teach tricks to other dolphins.

WOW! facts
Only whales, dolphins, elephants, apes and magpies can recognise themselves in a mirror.

Clever dolphins

A dolphin in the USA called Kelly was given a fish each time she picked up rubbish in her tank and gave it to a keeper.

She started to push each piece of paper rubbish under a stone and tear bits off. It meant she got a fish for every tiny scrap!

One dolphin in a sea-life park learned tail-walking just by watching other dolphins. She had never been trained to do it.

Our closest animal relatives

Gorillas and chimpanzees are primates, like humans. They are very clever, and often use tools.

- Gorillas use sticks to test how deep water is. They use tree-trunks as bridges if water is too deep to cross.

- Some monkeys strip the leaves from sticks and use the sticks to 'dip' for insects.

- Chimpanzees use sticks to break open beehives to reach honey.

- Chimpanzees make sponges from leaves and moss to soak up water, either to drink or to wash themselves.

- Some types of monkey use sharpened sticks to catch bush-babies or fish to eat.

Do you floss your teeth to clean them?

Macaque monkeys in Thailand pull hair from human visitors and use it to floss between their teeth.

They even show their babies how to do it.

5. PROBLEM SOLVING

Some animals are very good at solving problems.

Getting in and out

Crows are very clever birds. In Japan, crows have been seen dropping nuts onto the road and waiting for traffic to break the shells.

Super-smart crows drop the nuts at traffic lights. They wait for the traffic to break the nuts – and then they wait for the lights to change so that it's safe to pick up the pieces!

An octopus can open a jar by unscrewing the lid with its tentacles. It can even do this from the inside of the jar!

An octopus can also learn its way through a maze to get to food. And it can recognise signs and remember which sign is on a door that hides food.

Smarter than us?

Scientists tried an experiment with an orangutan.

They put a peanut at the bottom of a narrow glass tube. The orangutan couldn't reach it – but worked out a clever plan. She filled her mouth with water, then spat it into the tube. The peanut floated to the top.

The scientists tried the same test with people, using a sweet at the bottom of the tube. No one thought to use water!

WOW! facts

Crows do something similar. They will drop stones into water to make the water level rise until they can reach a floating treat.

Crows will also choose tools to reach treats.

One crow used three tools in a row:
- a short tool to reach a medium tool
- the medium tool to reach a long tool
- the long tool to hook a treat out of a tube

No other animal has been seen to use three tools in sequence.

All different

We often forget how smart animals can be because they can't talk to us, but they have many different gifts:

- working together
- learning about their surroundings
- communicating with each other
- making and using tools
- planning ahead

They show us that there are lots of different ways to be clever - whether you are a human or an animal.

Questions

How do fire ants save their eggs if their nest is flooded? *(page 7)*

Which type of animal makes a home from spit? *(page 13)*

Which type of bird teaches her unhatched chicks a password? *(page 18)*

What might you find hidden in a coconut shell dropped in the sea? *(page 21)*

Name two animals that use sponges as tools. *(pages 22 and 24)*

How can an orangutan get something out of a tube that is too narrow for its fingers? *(page 28)*

Index

ants 6, 7, 14
apartments 12
Australian fairy wren 18
catfish 19
chicks 17, 18
chimpanzees 24
China 13
coconut shells 21
crows 26, 28, 29
communicate 22
cuckoo 16, 17, 19
dolphins 22, 23
eggs 7, 15, 16, 17, 18, 19
gorillas 24
hermit crab 10
igloos 10
insects 14, 24
Legoland 10
log cabin 10
Macaque monkeys 25
millipedes 6
mound 14
mouth brooding 19
nests 7, 12, 13, 15, 16, 17
octopuses 20, 22
orangutan 28
password 18

recognise 22, 27
reed warbler 17
scientists 28
seagulls 8
shell 10, 11, 20, 21, 26
successful 5, 20
swiftlet 13
tail-walking 23
termites 14
tools 20, 24, 29, 30
wasps 15
weaver bird 12
whales 9
worms 8